COLLECTED POEMS

❧ George Abbe

BOOKS BY GEORGE ABBE

Poetry

Wait for These Things · 1940
Letter Home · 1944
The Wide Plains Roar · 1954
Bird in the Mulberry · 1954
The Incandescent Beast · 1957
Collected Poems · 1961

Fiction

Voices in the Square · 1938
Dreamer's Clay · 1940
Mr. Quill's Crusade · 1948
The Winter House · 1957
One More Puritan · 1960

Play

The Adomatic Man · 1960

Editor

Hill Wind: *The Letters and
Poems of Charles K. Abbe* · 1935

COLLECTED

 # POEMS

1932-1961

George Abbe

Richard · R · Smith

PETERBOROUGH · NEW HAMPSHIRE

Published by
The Richard R. Smith Co., Inc.
Peterborough, N. H.

Printed in the United States of America
by the Cabinet Press, Milford, N. H. and
bound by the Colonial Press Inc., Clinton, Mass.

This book is set in Linotype Granjon.

To C. T. Lloyd

Remembering the first poetic insights,
excitement, and dedication to the art

❧ NOTE ON ARRANGEMENT

The poems in this collection are arranged in three parts. The first part, consisting of new poems, follows no chronological pattern. In the second and third parts the poems appear in reverse order of their creation, the last poem in the book being the earliest.

ACKNOWLEDGMENTS

The author wishes to express his thanks to the following publications, in whose pages many of these poems first appeared, for permission to include them in the present volume:

Periodicals:
ACCENT: Penny and Fire. AMERICAN MERCURY: Black Lake. AMERICAN POETRY MAGAZINE: Thirst and a Dog Running; Summer Meadow. ANTIOCH REVIEW: The Hockey Forward and Mankind; A Waitress I Coveted; The First Dream: the Garage. THE ATLANTIC: The Harbor Longs for Shouting; Apples Immortal; Horizon Thong; The Animal; The Icehouse; The Giants. BLUE GUITAR: The Dye Works: Liberation. CALIFORNIA QUARTERLY: Early Morning Bus in Autumn. CHICAGO REVIEW: Elderly Tutor. COLORADO QUARTERLY: Child Nurture; The Tractors. EPOS: Water; Electric Toaster; The Blow; The Will to Die. FLAME: The Sanctuary. KALEIDOGRAPH: The Lineman. LADIES' HOME JOURNAL: I Saw an Army (Copyright 1960

by The Curtis Publishing Company). LYRIC: Trees from the Dead; Entreaty. NEW MEXICO QUARTERLY REVIEW: The Invaders; The Tennis Player. NEW ORLEANS POETRY JOURNAL: Underground; The Incandescent Beast; From the Motionless Twig. NEW REPUBLIC: Telephone Wires in Winter; The Idealist, The Barber; The Birds of Autumn. THE NEW YORK HERALD-TRIBUNE: Injunction; New York City. THE NEW YORK TIMES: Mountain; The Quarry; Red-Winged Blackbird. THE POET (Glasgow): The Canoe; The Book. POETRY: Alder Red: Little We Knew; New York Subway; The Bridge; The Passer; Halfback in the Open. POETRY CHAP-BOOK: Bird in the Mulberry. POETRY DIAL: A Skill in Killing; I, the Childless One. PRAIRIE SCHOONER: Death Is a Little Thing; The Power Plant (University of Nebraska Press). THE PROVIDENCE JOURNAL: On Growing Slightly Older. QUICKSILVER: The Lone, Immortal Car. SAN FRANCISCO REVIEW: The Diver. SATURDAY REVIEW: Remembered Cat; Sunset and Immortality; Possessor's Pity; A Fat Man Dies; The Nourishment of Memory; Blueberry Girl; Mint; The Hand-Car; The Expiation; Pizzicato. SOUTHWEST REVIEW: The Violation; The Ancient Dwelling; Fairway of Dedication; Hunter with a Jagged Mouth. SPARROW: Changed. VOICES: Immolation in July. WHETSTONE: The Skull; Helmeted Madonna. THE WINDOW (Great Britain): The Top of My Car, a Hand, a Keeper.

Books:

BIRD IN THE MULBERRY: by George Abbe, published by Marshall Jones Company, 1954.

COLLEGE VERSE: Prophecy; Henry; The Storekeeper; Departure — published by the College Poetry Society of America (1931-1941), and reprinted in TRIAL BALANCES, edited by Ann Winslow, published by the Macmillan Company, 1935.

PRISMATIC VOICES: Last Patch of Snow; The Color of a Flower — an anthology published by the Falcon's Wing Press.

WAIT FOR THESE THINGS: by George Abbe, published by Henry Holt & Co., 1940.

❧ CONTENTS

III · THE THAWING FIRE   1932-1949

COLLECTED POEMS

❧ George Abbe

I

 ❧ *The Yeast of Summer*

1958-1961

THE HAND-CAR

Down railroad track,
pumping the hand-car,
I came with a lump
of sun in my pocket,
a boys'-camp medal
stiff on my chest.

The yeast of summer
had swollen the woods to a feast
of lustful, blazing leaves.
Fleeing from instructors
in camping and rowing, I rushed
down the rusted, long-abandoned track.

It veered through mountain rock.
The shock of a straight-away
laced me cold; I saw
the long-unused railroad station; and there
with a fur about her neck,
and sad, accusing eyes,
my mother, watching me.

Pumping, I passed,
not letting my gaze leave the track.
The black, rusted metal rails rushed
under the hand-car's wheels
that screamed with rust.

There was a town without rooftops,
there was a town without towers,
and down between walls without cover
the sunlight tumbled pure;
and all through the bursting autumns
the wild leaves drifted their floors.

But winter, their winter was wisdom;
their heroes grew quickly then:
they ate at ice-deep tables
with fists like frozen rain;
their eyes were the lightning of rivers
beneath storms of skating men.

And when they stood for conversing,
majestic and patient-browed,
snow-haired and frosty-templed,
they flexed like roots in ground,
and flashed their glances wide.

Till all their rooms were pygmied;
they leaned on the tops of walls,
looked down on the streets below them,
tiny and drifted and still,
and trembled the borealis
with their own fierce, arctic yell.

THE FIRST DREAM: THE GARAGE

I kept telephoning the repairman at the garage. "Explain:
when will my car be ready?" And yet there,
staring out of a phone-booth, I stood, — there
in the very garage I was telephoning to.

"My dog," I said. "My luggage. Are they
safe? Locked in? What was wrong? Why
did I leave the car?"
The garageman's voice, thin and far, cracked like a celluloid
toy. I couldn't hear a word.

I hurried from the booth. The garage had many levels.
I kept striding down, down, searching.
There were burning-black cables and ancient cars being raised;
straining men held up cylinder-blocks.
I pushed through dangling cables and chains;
crazed, I sought everywhere, I ran.
But none was the repairman, none my car.
Wherever it stood, helpless and spent,
my dog was inside, all
my belongings.

I flung myself into another booth; my voice
boiled in the mouthpiece, under the close roof, like scalding
water: "Which part
of the garage are you in?
Is it fixed? The dog, you say, is gone?
The luggage was never there?"
I stared through my sweat, past
the scratched and grimy phone-booth glass; and tall

and horrifying hung cranes and chains and cables,
a forest through which
the click of the repairman's voice seemed to come,
humming into the phone over long wire, too far,
too tired. "I can't tell you how to get
to this level. I don't know what's wrong with your car.
The doors are unlocked and the luggage and dog
are gone."

THE NOURISHMENT OF MEMORY

A gentle master came to here;
he cut a small loaf from the air,
he sliced a cool taste from the green
of shadow hanging in the trees.

Before my unbelieving eyes
from cupboards of exquisite praise
shaped by the birds who frame the day,
he took my meat, he gave to me.

And was I strong? And did I shout?
My master's skin was pleasure-brown;
his eyes recalled the great fish lost
below the bridges of my past.

And yet, and yet the wish he gave
made me, a moment, weak to live;
the flesh and firm of this wild food
broke shock across my hidden blood;

until, through grief I felt my veins
swell with the corpuscles of sun;
until, through pain I sensed the fire
I owe dominions of the pure.

I saw an army coming against the sun.
Its men were faceless and its banners dead.
No cheering voice was lifted — no, not one.
The broken flesh of wounds forgot to bleed.

Upon their shields they bore their children's limbs
Seared in the oven of atomic glare;
Their belts were fission; and their armor gleam
The dust of blasts beyond the stratosphere.

Pricked was their skin and threaded white with steel;
The flame of rockets writhed along their thighs;
A chemistry of missiles bent the knee
And clothed the sorrowing mouth, the darkened eye.

Yet in their ranks they marched upon the sun,
With hands hung weaponless, with cindered cheek,
And spectral footstep faint as desert wind
That fails before it finds the strength to speak.

From death, the burning core of light, I watched,
And cried with soundless throat, "Beware! Beware!"
But deaf they moved, straight to what I had sought:
The fire of mastery, the target of power.

THE ANIMAL

That March had a neck like an animal;
its pussy-willow eyes watched me approaching.
O the snow in the tops of my boots, the melting water
cold through the rubber to my shins!
I think the taste of sky was threads of scarlet
cut round my body like glittering fever;
and I was breaking out my bones like steel
to reach and rake the last ice out of hills.

Over, over the meadows hiding their hair
under death till the whipping wind of June,
alone I dashed, approaching the wood I knew.
And there was that different animal, March,
meek with its pussy-willow eyes,
its neck of alder brown outstretched
to ask me to be merciful. I took
fewer than my sister had told me to. I hate
to break the body of March, to kill the living.

I came through sun
to touch the icehouse door,
the lintel framed in majesty
of shadow, the threshold beam
so deep it shook my heart.

I felt the branding iron of mountain light
glide from my back; I stood
in the blue-fountained shadow of a world.

Now, vaguely powerful monoliths
swathed in the sleep of sawdust time;
now, rhyming blocks of Grecian stone
frozen in habitudes of dream,
free me of the familiar's heat and blindness; let me
kneel upon the cold of all the rivered unpossessed:

the crested pillars of that Roman doom
long rooming now in crumbled underworlds:
the petals of Egyptian flowers
bowered in Everests of stone, in chill
of lips seduced to artifice,
the ice wherein the mastodons of fury fell
all fully armed, and wrapped in mystic valor.

Now pallor of light
at high, dim window, ancient beams,
the clear and aching violet of shadow.

The sun, the sun is gone! Alone
in cold I kneel, secure; and fail, and fall,

and stand to gaze
on seas of Vikings and Balboa, over deeps
beneath the last subliminal, beyond
the town's last fence and faltering, grassy rise.

O ice! O clothed in particles of wood
bled out of time,
your timeless is my mood,
your unfamiliar all my recognition and companionship.

Where I lectured, the platform was ankle-deep in water.
The crowded stadium soared, dimming from view.
The people read programs, laughed, played cards, ignored me.
Down the center aisle, ankle-deep water flowed;
the shoes of latecomers descending made no splash;
through diamond liquid, brown and black leather glowed.

My notes slid down into wet; I bent and shook them,
knew suddenly this was wrong lecture, crowd, and place.
Leaving by the center aisle, my shoes made no sound.
Down long meadows of shallow water I hurried, recalling
my love. I had betrayed her; but how and where?
Here, in the winters of youth, we had skied. Was this water
that melted world? Had she passed this way, fearing?

Now a dam, hissing, and thunder; but under it, canyons of dryness.
I walked far. I was naked on a vast beach.
There was no horizon, no water anywhere; I burned
with invisible sun. Then in that void of yearning
I felt arms about me. They were hers. But when I turned,
she kept at my back, behind me always. Violent,
I twisted, revolved; but always the soft arms clung;
she was there, but evaded. I stood on the sand,
the expanding and limitless beach, the wind cool; but I could not
face her, or ever draw her to where I could see.
There was no horizon; only wind without variation.

The birches slash at the shadow
With the pure white of joy;
the dark fir pour upward
to stain the mountain.

Out of the rocks come shouting,
immense, hospitable people,
hands like slabs of laughter,
hearts as gentle as moss.

To right and left they shower
all the coin in the world;
it lies like slag in the foothills,
like lustreless ash.

Up icy streams they stride,
breaking trout in their fists,
bugling to thrush and sparrow:
"No money! Not ever again!"

And out of the village doorways,
drunken and blazing with mirth,
shining like metal with glory,
the people pour to greet them,

no purse, no past, no guile;
only an open tumbling
caught and buried in bigness
illimitable.

I'm not sure why I touched it.
A crocus-tip can be more dazzling,
and a boy would rather throw dice
or marbles than be soft-hearted.

But the snow was the last,
in a corner between tree and wall.
The far crow answered things I had never asked,
and the wind, nearly April, moved
the buds. I almost remembered what I'd felt
in the long blizzard; I nearly recalled
the power of my legs driving the skis.

Or was it the thought of a kitten, white,
who slept under earth I'd turned
myself in spring, a corner of the garden
withdrawn and secret, where, shaken,
the white wild cherry blossom fell?

I cannot tell. But I knelt
as I did when told, in older people's prayer,
and taking the snow upon my palm,
saw the warmth of sun turn it to water,
the shudder and tremble, a tingling light.
I heard the crow, crying toward the river land,
the corn to fall, the hot suns of tomorrow;
and sorrow older than my memory flowed
from the fierce cold into my palm's blood.

and to each breast she strained
a babe just born.
And one was myself,
puckered and doubled in sorrow;

and one, with a buzzard's eye
and a broken neck,
was the child I have never fathered,
cold blue as the shadow of mountains.

Through the hanging turkey's mouth
I drove a needle in,
straight up into its brain.

I felt the tissue give;
the will to live
ran scarlet on my hand;
and the breathing beak
gaped at my work.

Revolted, I forced myself.
This was the neatest way,
science had said: strike
the needle deep,
up through the mouth's roof;
the nerves are paralyzed,
the feathers made loose.
But as I probed and drove,
the tissues of my brain
broke with a thought that moved,
a pin-prick gentle as love.
Yet, numb, I could not feel.
Not method nor resolve
made the act real.

By the gray river,
by the grim rock,
a few children hurried,
a woman lay down.

A man left his shadow
at his doorway and came;
the sheep watched a moment,
the bees crowded home.

What colored the cloud-land
with a joy of the mute?
The children grew pensive,
the man ran and stood

by the woman, and kneeling,
unfastened her clothes;
the bees stilled each other;
the sky became stone.

On the slow river floated
orange peel scraps,
an ice cream carton,
and a mustard stick.

They lodged in the rock;
the woman stood up;
the children's beauty
delighted the sheep.

BOYHOOD LAKE REVISITED: A GLIMPSE OF IMMORTALITY

An architect designs the tensile light
striking through lakes of youth in planes of fire
that waver, melt, and break to glittering wool,
a spool of gold undone, the flickering stone
clean as the ankle of a goddess
calling me close. Voices of friends I hear:
the fearful tones of arcing thunder
flung from rock hill over and down
on water-pavement blocked in wind and mosaic of rain.

The pools once stunned by the fisher's hook
look kindly up at me.
I see the trout we never caught
rocking in sleep, the skater's foot
set in the flash of speed.
Greedy and crude, that bulky Alden laughs,
crashing door-panels with his fist, blowing
holes in the dump-heap with a birthday gun.
My clumsy, dawn-cold fingers comb the berries
scurrying down the heavy-breaking waves of high-bush blue.
And light flames on our sail-boat, the mountain
shouts venture and welcome like a black, hard-arching
star. The water folds and cuts the light;
bright waver the stones I walked in my first swimming.

We live the structured air, the running deeds of time
that writhe and bend into reflected gleam,
shining descend to shape a solemn thought.
All greatness due us is already built, and where
stairways climb down we made our ladders before.

The architect reverses window and act that we may find,
winding, refracted, in the watery light,
our lives to be — clearly inverted in the flashing depth
like every episode that sinews the mortal house:
the oriels and fierce facades of later worlds
called forth in flicker and supple-curve and shade
of moods and moments instinct-kept
in lakes of here.

Those hills flow downward out of darkest time,
rent by the tree-trunks of the unperceivable
whose branches are the long-forgotten flame
that blossoms in the deserts of the soul.

And down and downward falls the earth of day
to the deep-bright, to the deep-coiling water,
and I see heroes standing to their knee
in the cold depths, in the rushing horror
of all that they recall and conquer here
in the roiling river of valleys lending power.

And birds drift down, and the ferns of the alone
flicker and wing through brightness over stone.

And suddenly, from the curved floor, from the doubt's ending,
I see the people bursting upward to their source,
and upward they flow, hero and spirit of tree-trunk sending
the glad strength of the dreamer recalling that thirst
which is the womb, the core, the heart of glad beginnings,
which is the summit and the incredible first
wrapped in the inviolate and the divine,
the turmoil, the down-rushing, and the green.

Harsh, strong, and dark as crows
they flow to plant the earth.
Their lax and gentle clicking
of tongue between their beaks
is warm with mother urge.

Out of their wombs the flowers
of wheat and people strive,
rising to gleam and live
as noble as these feathers

of metal, as quick with sense
as piston-muscles firm
in oil of grace, and cam
and valve deathless with dance.

To margin of man's river
the swarms that seed our flesh
with plunder of happiness,
their heart the carburetor

hushing the blood, their wings
the blue-black span of fender
beating through dust and sun.
I watch, and I am strong.

He made love to water
the way we did to girls.
Hard-limbed, he climbed the tower,
black-haired and fair,
his hair a tight-curled helmet
fierce-bright with iron curls.
Handsome he poised, the drops
fell from his crotch.

A slow and perfect dive.
He could stay under
longer than any: two minutes,
or more, slipping along
wave-bend and bubble, caressing
lingering grass. He thumbed
the nipple of sun
subaqueous, stroked the thigh
of light-slant bottom-deep;
he kissed the eyes,
the mouth of spring-fed cold,
and parted the knees of shadow
for gentle rape.

He was the handsomest, he
was the perfect diver;
he dove to stay and he came back
secret and stronger.

Last week, like the picked bones
of a perch, he died.
His side lay opened and carved back

time after time
for cancer to go in.
A pink grotto, it lay
for the waves of a diver to come;
and from clear sky,
the black helmet rushed,
the hard legs drove down.

Hard by my window, under the frost
of the last shadow of night,
a late and patient iris hung,
whose hope was my footstep, whose only star
the fair hand of my mercy that might permit her
to endure.

I drew the fragrance from her soul, I drained
the clear ardor of her skin,
and chilled my own impatience with the ice
of her wise meditation; and step by step I took
the good of her thought, the tincture of her flesh
and crushed her into withering with my want.

The frost of shadow covers again
the pain of day. I look to see
the gleam of iris for my sleeping.
Deep to the sands of absence she has gone,
brought under by my love, thrust down
by my lean and terrible desire
for the pure.

What tender wish could be defiled
with viler atavism? What trust broken
with grosser lust? Abandoned I sleep,
and dream of one betrayed
who rages beautiful as a leopard beyond
the wall where she shall face me when I die.

INJUNCTION

If I should fail the thought I love
and die before I reach the end,
then take the pillar of my blood
and sink it in the marsh of mind
and on it burn "Insanity."
For only madness speaks the hour,
and only horror can be free.
The yielding self alone is power.
Do not religions teach us that?
Submission is stronger than all wit.

Renunciation triggers forth
the life that crushes boredom's worm;
let drunken symbols stamp their wreath
on manhood's brow in honor's name.
From darkness let the hands essay;
from cold dementia light your gleam;
give in; serve some apostasy
whose diabolic itch is joy.

The child screamed at the brook's edge.
The water's subtle gleam
revealed a father standing calm,
the mother striking in rage.
The child's body, thin from food
parentally compelled,
strained toward the father's cynic cold,
hoping for hidden good.

But on his body, lean as the child's,
fresh marks of cancer fed;
all of his wife's most brutal bread
forced on the son had failed

likewise to give the father strength
or flicker of old love;
that tenderness the bridegroom gave
had weaned the bride away
to strict indifference to sex,

had borne him his pain of need,
till out of her sprang that disease:
all day, most beautiful and vexed,
to stand behind the son's chair
at meals, and scream, "You eat!
By God, you clean that plate!"
till the son wept with fear.

Now, to brook's edge he'd fled; the dusk
was milky with scent of flowers.

The mother had struck, till her son's tears
had dried, his will a husk;

and the father, dying himself from lack,
could not respond, or move;
the body of his cancer grew.
Most calm from being sick,
he yearned to touch his son, to break
the freezing and unspeakable,
the helpless, and too late.

I have just come back from the country
of hunted and tongueless people,
where the children's eyes are of sand,
their hands like running water;
and the long shape of their clothing
is the flow of wind in space.

Their faces were fragments of mine.
I felt their houses about me,
tall glancings of sun, no more;
their doors were the dew of silence,
the bright windows, pain.
In the rain of shadowy coolness
moved the pale breathing of parents;
but none knew who or where.

To an airy meadow came
for games of quiet and distance
the children, whose voices coiled
like gold railings of balustrades
patiently thin and lost
in a ghostly and beautiful past.
Their laughter abated like grass
that, trampled, will stir and fail.

Someone had flung a skull
on a mossy rock in their center;
in wonder they stood to watch
till the hot lime whiteness shone
with the bone of hoping and sorrow.

The narrow eye-sockets were mine;
dry and true were the teeth
with the death of my own first hungers;
the brain had lived to return.

The color of a flower is trying to say something to me;
is trying, is trying, burning and vibrating.
When I stare at it long, it dazzles me with the occult,
it blinds me with important language.
What is the color doing? What is it trying to say to me?
It is reaching out, more powerful than light-years;
it is racing toward me, swifter than comets.

I wonder if it is saying: I am the blood of meaning; I am the
    pulse of thought?
I will hold you and heal you? I am the final delight?

No. I find at last what it is thinking:
The color is only what I *will* it to be,
what I *decide* it is thinking.
And my decision is, my feeling of what is in the flower color
    is: life, vividness, immortal fraternity.
All these things *be* — *be* in that color — I think hopefully;
throb in it, be its idea;
eternity is valid, and we shall all be drawn there together,
exalted, vindicated — the color, I, everything.

And that is what the color is saying to me, then, —
just what I *will* the color to think,
just what I *am* and *hope* and *want,* reaching into the color.
After all, then, I do not have to *try* to find the thought of the color;
it helps *me* to find myself. It permits me to think
my own virtue and my truth.

II

Leap the Measured Arc

1950-1957

Two men in helmets of fury
struck at the power plant door,
their fists knuckled with gore.
Their armor shone bright and heavy.

Where the cold trees made no shadow
and mortal houses were deaf,
to the home of machinery's Pharoah
they came to converse of Now
and the tyrannies they had left
in the age of the spear and the barrow.

The power plant shook with turbine;
above, wires coiled with flame.
But their shouting was void of name;
their voices started no engine;
no living guardian came.

High chimney rolling its black
down hillsides rubbled and wan;
empty, the roadway leaned
toward forgotten vales of the meek,
soft murmurings lost to man.

Back from the door stood the warriors,
to the parapet's edge of steel
strode, and with noble wonder
saw looming the hunched transformers,
strung saucers glazed like tile,
white blaze of insulators,
the moaning high barbed wire.

And the roadway ran to the town.
Through the windows of homes they saw,
enormous, the joints of machines
elbowing fast and clean,
the switches enamelled and new
by mechanical fingers thrown;

lines of unspeaking children
clad only in copper belts
wound past parental tombs,
ascending from well-shaft gloom,
descending, having fed
the metal dwellers of homes

with their perfect sound, having poured
raw strength for the last great Word.

THE HOCKEY FORWARD AND MANKIND

Cutting, as will the saw within the wood,
the angry line to cleavage,
cool ice dust clouding the air,
the forward barrels against the grain of space,
breaking gnarled knots of rage —
checking defensemen heavy against his mood.

He guns the alley, is struck, staggers . . . and there,
there at net's mouth the crouched-and-padded waits;
and gathering teeth and blood he snaps the live blade,
the rubber, low and screaming across smoked light.

The white net takes it, yielding as girl's flesh might.
And swerving. . . stumbling at outer rim of shot,
he sees the crowd, instant with roaring, the scorer's red flash.

If we could hurl our present on future like this,
crowding on strength for devout and selfless dash,
some assault on terror and war's woe. . .
then. . . then the clicking win, the red bulb's kiss
could tell us man had sliced through smoky fear,
was harbored in white nets, the yielding flesh of peace.
The watching stars would roar, the universe cheer.

Now never never winter fire,
now never brick that warmed the tongue,
nor pristine hand on earthenware
the color of water and blown fir;

through halls where words died to a pulse,
where toys by careless feet were crushed,
the scent of baking dimly done
by hand scarcely remembered still
floats to the attic of old need;

in cellars where apples waited hushed,
the veins of buried light still bleed;
potato tendrils furtive thrill
to wood scraps harboring the heat
trapped once beneath the summer's heel;

dark holy phrases left by the thrush
perish along those family walls
where the brute mouths of dampness feed.

Flying in plane's rib,
cribbed and yearning for earth-touch birth,
watching, down-reaching, I saw worlds below
that intransigent city adrift by night,
bright-pulsed, flung-upward, flamed with silver,
white-fountained, love-finned, embossed by tumult.

The plane leaned, the city grew, rose to ensnare
brain's eye, blood's finger-tip, all desert hope.

Yet lovely far, yet hung like rose,
yet known to thirsty and the proud,
suspended out of time, ungeared
from mesh of soil and flesh and metal,

released, as was the angel from stone,
flown, out-flung as virtue's rocket
locked in God's dream, wistful as man.

His wife
tried to insist
he visit the art exhibit —
religion with her; with him, death.
Instead, he cursed her rapture, departed in anger;
took danger and lolling sea of afternoon lonely
strolling the golf course, under green flow
of slow sun wave, gold flower:
hours of devotion.

Soft
the lofty sail
of elm and cloud, and deep
his clean rubber soles on grass.
To pass the shrine of honeysuckle he bows
the cool Now of money enough, male strength
to lengths of abstract time,
far chime of truth:

And new
with reverent will,
spills the approach shot at brink
of green ring where satyrs kneel;
the steel and fire of Hera flow in his putt;
the rush of Artemis' arrow climbs
in his drive — falling on chapels
dappled with leaves
of dreaming.

Planned hook
past brook to green

is the freed spirit's stroke
broken to canvas. Titian's line
flies warm with shining in ball's curve and bound.
Soft mound of bunker, flash of ball from trap
catch meaning of memorial, and art.
The garb and air of Botticelli
lightly breathe in girl
who twirls club leaving tee,
free-moving.

Behold,
the gold of Raphael
falls on the distant surf;
the stuff of oratorio
flows on the Sistine of the living sky.
White blazes distant clubhouse by white beach,
teaching like Michelangelo,
toned like Madonna's chair
where bare love lies
in the arm
of bar and dance floor,
pure yacht sail and beach,
fresh chancel rock
for backdrop.

HUNTER WITH A JAGGED MOUTH

Could that day ever have brought the snow's end?
Would that hill have burned us down with its violet?
Tall bearer of guns whose chest was timber,
Spill the great snow at the knee with striding thrust.

West lay the forest. Could it bring the deer?
Hill lost beneath the star. Fir where the deer
stilled the torn heart. Bearer of sound
bound within rifle bore as mercy in rock,
mockery of mouth, call not the day back.
Could fear have heard? Could the ice
in wood have touched your hand or violet,
or the soft of fur where the blood stiffened?
What wind is bringing the snow down
from those boughs the same? What trail is twilight-greening
by the lean cabins and the food of the killed?
Come nearer, mocking and terrible giant
who jeered the gentle with hook of mouth,
the loud of scorn, whose rifle barrel,
jewel of your heat and caressing,
hissed in the crystal wild of night.

O giant, O houses gone with the evening lights,
the yellow dulled in the blowing. . . ! Could we know,
would we ever have come to that slope?
Could hoping, could urge have made
bravery out of roar and color and tendon yielding,
and the pleading hidden under the homeward bough?

THE SANCTUARY

O there below that violet mist
and windows flaming with that light no one can tell,
round silver dollars rolled on floors immense
and rolling upward, vast and steep as hills,

behind which, crouching, run those fearful men
who hold those silver dollars up as shields.
The streets have no walls, for the houses are flat
or tilted backwards into hedges thick with dust;
the men run, rolling the dollars like children's hoops
first over windows in which dead faces rest,
then down dry clapboards rattling with dim reproach.

Bridges are crossed where halves of bodies are hung,
the waters stiff with hands and ancient sinew.
Now flames that rolling silver with some departed sun
obliquely drained past arches of thin rust.

And now at church; they surround it, ease the coins
into a tall-slab circle farther than spire;
enter the pews, and in wild darkness hear
the silver beating of sound from high, high groin
where stained-glass windows cut from natural light
by rims of silver thickness receive new glow
from flesh of bells tolling the safe and true
in dusk made sanctified by common fate.

I heard a woman soft with fat
cry out she saw her husband dead,
that he had risen from his bed
a certain way, and, just like that,
had fallen, and when they lifted him
his limbs were lard, his heart a crumb.

I saw her, gentle and piteous,
whose fleshiness had melted his,
torn from her dream, and there upon
tomorrow's white and icy screen
he rose, he fell, he died the same
as in that most meticulous dream.

And now, her softness, large and giving,
yearned at his live obesity,
his kindness slow and darkly striving;
yet all her size could vainly do
was make his lips more certain gray;
with each caress his own fat grew;

till, sick, from their sad bed he rose,
and fell, and died as in her dream, —
with one thing added: he was so large
from life, from her, his burial mound,
big beyond custom, drew men's eyes
and gave them pause for miles around.

THE TENNIS PLAYER

His racket beat against the cliffs of heaven;
ball after ball burst in supernal smoke;
he hurled the power to kill, to be forgiven;
air was a sheaf of atoms that he woke.

The lines he raced were boundaries of the sun,
and where he crossed a thunderous image burned;
the net was choir, the clay a subject land;
his images taught the galaxies to shine.

Along his arm the purest mercy flowed,
to sanction virtue of the sharp return,
to end his enemy with quickest blow.

What became of her? I recall the hot boards
of the boathouse dock, the canoe drawn up,
polished, like a knife fallen from the hip
of an Indian; the sound of cicadas was a cord
drawn against the heaviest arteries of the body;
and my hand had found her flesh, and her eyes stared.

Where did she go? And the boy who loved her,
as I never did? That village was lonely;
its hotel, on the highest hill, burned.
Its farms, desperate, dying, ugly,
festered upon the inner will. For each disease
of tree or heart, some mortal suffers.
Stretched on the hot boards, her white, closed knees
fighting my hand like celery reluctant to tear, —
what corrupt thing did she see in me? What fear
hurling its converse, violence, to compensate?

The sun went down. Across the sorrowing lake
the cattails' ragged silhouettes, dreamingly seen. . . .
like parents dead, or mutter of an old machine
that sews a dress long since discarded, shadowy.
We paddled homeward, wordless, passion the scales
of a fish floating, belly up, in the boat's wake.
Whippoorwill's voice came cold. Our laughter was faked.

Shiny and livid and steaming with odor — a pile
of organs ripped from a fowl — up there ahead
lay the village, for us forever the savage and vile.
And what was marriage if friendship could never begin?
Where are her children? To what dark has she fled?
Does she feel my lust in the boredom of other men?

At the beautiful instant of gratification,
my cry spiralling as hurricane
among the high flowers of your skin,
winning, but losing, that fragrance poured
from the storeroom of your blood,
the budding bees
of sweetness stinging me to rage —

in that inviolate trance
I flash outward beyond believing,
down green slopes of art and theatre
and rearing cross, bright grass, and all devised
by mind of mortal to adorn.
Torn from their pretense, they coil
down, away, to an insect sigh.

And I, run with dinosaurian stride
to the wide arch, the bridge,
the livid span to university hill:
tall Doric arch, and wisdom looking out.

With shout of you-and-I, I duck and raise
my glazed-gold-armored head of primal
rioting, and tear the bridge asunder,
in wonder see the slopes of learning,
the stadium of time
dying, and feel splinters of raptured water
shatter upward to my knee
with a free man's light.

Dropping back with the ball ripe in my palm,
grained and firm as the flesh of a living charm,
I taper and coil myself down, raise arm to fake,
running a little, seeing my targets emerge
like quail above a wheat field's golden lake.

In boyhood I saw my mother knit my warmth
with needles that were straight. I learned to feel
the passage of the bullet through the bore,
its vein of flight between my heart and deer
whose terror took the pulse of my hot will.

I learned how wild geese slice arcs from hanging pear
of autumn noon; how the thought of love cleaves home,
and fists, with fury's ray, can lay a weakness bare,
and instinct's eye can mine fish under foam.

So as I run and weigh, measure and test,
the light kindles on helmets, the angry leap;
but secretly, coolly, as though stretching a hand to his chest,
I lay the ball in the arms of my planing end,
as true as metal, as deftly as surgeon's wrist.

I entered a subway at bleeding noon.
Its waiting caves were ribbed with dust;
its sweating metal empty shone;
faintly its motors beat with remorse.

Four men entered, never known
in any country where I'd been.
The long cars started, as in pain;
the dark whirled by with ultimate haste.

And one cried: "No, I cannot stop!"
and dashed the windows through with fists;
another, bending through a trap,
let the fast wheels cut through his wrists.

Another, leaping to a seat,
stretched downward, holding to a strap;
of terror and repentance preached,
though nothing heard nor turned to wait.

And last, the fourth, lofty and hard,
with cheeks of basalt slashed by thought,
raced to the car-end, struck the door,
the steel that smoldered with friction's flame.

"O motorman! O name the track,
the station, and the usual fare!"
His hands clung; he could not pull back;
clothing and flesh broke open and streamed
against that sucking steel blown hot,
against that tiny window black
with tunnel coming, no human there.

Go back now; pause to mark
that hill town cut in two:
one half, green summer's charm,
the other, chasmed in snow.
Horizon, a thong of red
knotted by smoldering sun;
wind, the wind in the drifts,
and crystal blossoms flung
downward — so near, so warm —
to where orchards bend and lift.

And father, — father who kneels
to pull snowshoes from his back,
looks down to the shining field
where his son runs, easy and fast;

he must follow, follow to save,
but the snowshoes will not free;
they are rooted to shoulder blade,
they are flesh of paternity.

Only a quick run down,
but helpless he kneels in cold,
watches his young boy run
over meadows lyric and full
towards woods, a woods of his own.

Wrenching, and wet with pain,
the father downward bows;
the village of homes and men
grows faint in the blizzard's glow.

The boy flashes under trees
and fades. The horizon mark
binds throat of man on his knees;
the sun-knot tightens to dark.

TO THAT STAIRWAY I CAME

To that stairway I came where low the shadow lay
of hands and inward flame and grace to climb the same
by bannister light-warmed as the wide arms of come,
to rooms dressed all unharmed, in act of childhood done.

Dear door and window glass gemmed at the breast of night
through which I saw hope's flesh and forms of thirst in flight;
satanic well of stone cupping the parent depth;
wind severed from its own — the shape of branches left.

At brink of upward self, on threshold tilting in,
open, O known regret, the hour that made me man
before the child was dead.

THE LONE, IMMORTAL CAR

Take, now, the lone, immortal car;
bar from all roads the rest;
press holy foot to pedal, shock forward far
to west, to sliding south,
dry-mouthed, and springing flame on head.

Can you see, alone, the country is more sane?
The rain of heaven beats upon your dust;
love is the rising fir, and motor hush,
roads shorn
of mortal, staring
with bare eternal evenness
of speech. For here the empty
teaches, and the eye can search
time's work within the wheel of here,
fearless with God's care.

Burn the white gas of pensive speed.
Agree. Agree to be singular and fleeing
and at rest
with the vast, barren road.
Goad the late heart with steel-precision hurry
that carries the one car, mortal-redeemed
to verge of grace
And trace, O trace your fine tires in the
endless dust!

The air grieved and the island
died at the edge of sun.
From the clubhouse the wealthy swam
toward the mountain's blue fan,
toward its shade and its dim.

Spring water shocked their blood:
in the channels of cold they slowed;
they recalled words like "should";
from underground years there flowed
forgotten torrents of good.

A girl with a blueberry pail
strapped to a belt of fire
came out of a brushland trail,
her blue-smeared mouth and hair
coarse with the bayberry smell
and the taste of the deep-earth choir.

Her breasts were circles of garnet
budded to green speech,
the down of her hand a linnet
bending the harp of the birch,
and out of her eyes and flesh
she sent the moth of her kiss.

The men broken by golf course,
skewered on heat of court,
waited with eyes like a dead purse
opened to show their hurt;
their swimming died at its source,

between boredom's better and worse,
their wet arms fixed to doubt.

Now bright to the listening water
she came where mountain shadow
blurred her to fairer and better,
and the curve of her throat was a cello
plucked in the twilight gather;

and when she bent to fill
the sharp white of her pail,
the swimmers felt fear still,
felt coldness temper and fail.

Her garnet breasts drank light
as her blueberry mouth drew wet;
the swimmers' hearts turned hot,
their eyes and the drinker's met;

and rage of the blueberry noontime,
the temples of mountain fir,
the sawdust ant and the bee chime
came stinging out of her.

They sank, and sinking heard
her innocent murmuring lips —
lost bell from the clubhouse deck
calling them back to the church
of their comfort, their profiting work.

Deep land which curves the mystic slopes
to windows of worlds we knew before
and will know yet, more ample and pure,
where constellations are willow smoke
in spring of time, by seaward creek,
where grazes the lamb of lightning stroke
and thunder's birds feed from the hand;
youth's flower, hopes meadow flaming steep;
those fragment voices rising blind
up hills where trembles mercy's bough;
lost wind below our guilty sleep.

FROM THE MOTIONLESS TWIG

This wisdom I learned from the motionless twig:
there is no place to go, and haste is illusion.
The things I would fashion from small into big
are already as large as my heart could have chosen.
And what I believed I could master was there,
precisely achieved in the act of my prayer.

Why fear? Why reach out?
I am here. I am done.
For movement means only a doubt.
The world I will shape to my resting:
no light will fly out from the sun;
no petal will blow from the bough;
the storm will drive not the cloud,
will be always arresting.

There is nothing but now,
and whatever's begun is through,
and each hope I enlisted has won.

THE INCANDESCENT BEAST

A dog lay dead in village square,
yet dead it did not die entire:
in rain, its muzzle shone like glass,
in blowing leaves, the haunches stirred.
Kind villagers who left it there
loved it as something oddly blest:
their own, their lost, their lonely-fair.

A boy with candy ball on stick,
a ruby sweet, wet-bright from tongue,
paused longest to regard the black
pure licorice of the dog's smooth paw.
Light came from outer mountain range
to kindle what he tasted and saw:
slick candy taste made godly and strange,
the beast made glowing as words of love.
And beryl was that sleeping fur,
and topaz the enlivened eye;
clear as a fire its torpid musk,
and people passing knew it changed,
yet changing, it was ever thus.

So one of beard and older-framed,
to the sick, ever-sanguine beast
gently, with a wise hand came
and brushed the cold fur from its face,
and saw the naked teeth were gems.

The boy came closer, fell to knee
and held his ruby candy near

that prism through which flashed the sky
past all perceived, clairvoyant clear,
and flesh more aboriginal
than death blazed color to his trust,
his prism of deep-dreaming best.

The mountain borrows hunger from the wind;
it broods upon the finished flesh of time,
the aboriginal decay of hills,
dead birds of stars, and twilight's slaughtered hind.

Think not, in climbing to its noble arc,
that it knows not the burning of our need;
the pulse of rock is veined with heaven's dark,
the mountain stretches love when mortals bleed.

THE TOP OF MY CAR, A HAND, A KEEPER

A clear, a clean a very clean hand, a roll
of sheath of shine to keep the inner soul
to keep the warm car mine;
now feel it, driving, shunting wind, I praise
the sun it curls, the wind it slides, the days,
the sun, the whirl, it wraps my praise.

You can profoundly drive more easily,
on wheel, on puff of air and rubber's elbow stroll
if God gives car top to your careful soul,
a metal better than crusader's mail.

Bless it, oh glad my top, my curving, my round!
Bless Jesus' hand, his palm that shapes it mine!
He made the worker who made press and hammer and heat.

Dear sound
of motor, wine in cup of going, communion divine;
warm lips of speed, clean needed rest, God's wound.
The car top held the ice, it broke July.

Stroll, curve, and smooth. Surround! With God I fly
under this sly cap, hiding and keeper of joy,
connecting sky air and flexing, rolling ground.

Water fails us never, no, nor falters.
Smother love, but never turn from water.
By the harvest columns of youth's grasses
sky-gleam and brook.

Frog and chipmunk live reflected daily;
log is buoyant made to hide the trout-child;
numb my legs with swim of every pleading.
Come, water, bless me.

Out from forest loved as templed hiding,
trout within your shining palm, and shadow,
teach a facile yielding to time's contour.
Reach me with music.

Monument and bridge the water brushes,
bridges plucked from mind and smoothed with handling.
Dawn and heron are born only from water.
Live with me, father.

Owls know well the night, when water is hidden;
cowards can never trace the green to its source;
deep is the damp the twisted mesquite knows.
Seek me, far under.

Thirst is heavy-bound in mortal sinew.
Flow me, blend me, loosen me forever.
When I scatter in the dusts of terror,
water, unite me.

I came to the margin of yesterday;
I saw a girl on the edge of flowers.
There were birds on a steeple, and clouds as high
as the stars of childhood in mystery's tower.

A gray stone library, red of roof,
stood by a sidewalk where people were small
but excessively kind, and their voices drew
the fish from the water, the fox from the hill.

The girl on the edge of the flowers stood deep,
so deep in the grass I saw only her head
and a bare arm held high. She looked rosy and sweet.
Then I saw what she held — a book she had read,
far down in the insects, the drowsing, the pollen.
The words she had read shone like drops on her brow
and glowed on her lips, and exquisitely shone
in eyes blue-eternal and gray here-and-now;

and from library windows, heads were thrust out,
the steeple birds paused, and the clouds swung low;
the fox raised his head, the fish made no sound;
the flowers were diamonds from the darkest unknown.

Riding
behind a man,
hand clasped on a silver bar,
fur-seated, booted, breeches of cord,
sword of the light on her studded belt, her shirt
purple and nacreous-buttoned under the jacket,

she floats
the motorcycle
aisle of stunning grace,
the racing narrows between cars,
hard smell of oil and pavement and leaning danger.

Braver,
being male and leader,
flees rigid driver before her,
thorn of his eyes to wind, the proud
glad swell of sinew, the master's seed in his loin.

And she,
freely, with hunger
offers her tender hiding to his
high skill, pressing her cheek, eyes closed, to his back.

But wait!
No hair of angel
ranges the wind behind,
no flying benediction seraphic;
the traffic girl dwells deep in a helmet of black,

so huge,
the blue shadow
of brow, the chin's shy dip,
the lips meek and devout seem
to beseech escape, too soft for this Jovian ravaging.
And then,
swung to the gas station
for patient eucharist
of hi-test fuel, the cycle stands,
commanding all eyes with its exalted glitter;

the girl
uncurling from
submission, steps to earth,
tugs girth of flashing leather, shoves
jutting curve of helmet high and back,

then slacks
the arc of breasts,
and resting, lounges, draws
from pocket, king-size cigarette,
flexes her lips, her eyes grown coldly laughing.

"This stuff
and love don't mix!
Cricks in my neck! God!
My crotch aches like a broken back!"
She laughs. Spits. Caresses the arm of her man.

She was afraid of bushes. She could never cross
any field where bushes leaned alone and hot
under the naked muscle of the sun.
She was alone and frightened and undone,
and hurried the streets where pavements were a friend,
and thought of cool meals in a placid room.

The children she tutored reminded her of men —
all the nice men she had liked but never married.

But she could not explain why bushes broke her down,
why, on the neat wedgewood plate of summer day as she hurried,
whenever at the corner of her eye
loomed the glutton-eater, the fleshy shape of bushes,
wherever they were and of whatever kind —
faintly she twitched like the drawn skin of a wound.

The Lord's face is an axe-head
sharp gray and able,
fierce as breath from the dead,
more living than my hand,
spiked into a fresh white handle.

I am the log that is split,
the mold, the wood's decay
simply, murderously torn.

Descending from its poise,
down with a savage virtue,
fact-hard and loving-sure,
furious to learn how I endure
so long bound in my own choice,
so long dying in my own tissue,

the axe-head knows its debt,
and how that debt is paid;
the rot of the log lies cut,
the axe-head staring me cold,
and under I see gray rock
which the axe-head struck
with good sound, with live spark.

THE DYE WORKS: LIBERATION

Colors in vats become
the round and singing dome
of the sky's clear room;

we break aside the cell
of textile and chemical,
stand manlike and love-full.

Hands that are scoured of stain
by sun of quicker grace
we lift in honor's name

to all who pass.
The flesh dyed in the vat
clothes truthful man;

color of labor shines
town-bright, as yours, as mine,
mortal-divine,

as terribly like song
as streets we dance along
where power for all

hangs vivid in bright trees,
bursts from the anguished days
when on our knees

we took the acid's fire
in flesh cut by the fear
of time-card and buyer.

HALF-BACK IN THE OPEN

Good half-back, sprung to open field,
the shoulders high and fierce,
blue helmet like iridescent oil
on streets where sun is terse,

carry the hard canter of my anger
which I cannot spend against cities;
rowel the frozen earth with rancor
that dies in my heart as pity.

Carry my feeble, broken brain
made imbecile by fear;
hurl it on burning prongs of pain,
torn mouth and scalding air.

On touchdown rampart break my mood,
the frustrate and unused;
when cleat cuts fallen foe to blood,
gore me with your reproof.

Thunder the death of what I fear:
the debt, the mocking wage,
all love made eunuch by endless war.
In one hard fury purge

the stale bile at my lips, the foul
terror of guilty night;
hurl, hero; speed, brutal and cool,
to the last line's sinless white.

Death is a little thing:
You can put it in a box;
in the dust of an insect wing
it makes an eager spot.

You can catch it in the gleam
of wetness on a lip.
From a sentence born to death
a word may bend and lean: —
and that is darkness' ship,
and that the grave to be.

You can cage it in the corner
in a wink of sun.
Death is a furled banner
with war begun;

on thrush-sad summer road
in quiet rain,
from under a crushed bird's body
the faintest stain;

the fleck of lily powder
on casket's rim
that falls between lid lowered
and music that has been.

Because I bleed with memory, with love
in the ripe orchard of summer, some gentle seed
of grass will be more free, some aging tree
will draw the glove of wind with greater pride
over its hand, to take one final walk
on paths of flowering delight with birds and me.

Because I care and suffer without words,
the valleys far and city-quick
and deep and sweet with fruits of long-gone youth
will glow with martyr's lustre in the night,
will be the resurrection of my flesh,
the pleasures I must finally leave,
the bright weight of my old desires
made manifest by insect fire
and citadels of mortal flame.
And the scent of cut hay which will bear my name
spirals more beautifully because my breath expires.

When you see the traffic light
brighten with red, and reach
the clear thorn of warning far,
starring the city air, — then there,
there is the quince bush within whose flare
the tired driver plunges flesh:
the mesh of Christ, no less, the love
swung forth from wires and poles of grace.
No face of Jesus rose more clear
to bare the fault, to still the weary.
He cared for traveller whose eyes looked up.
Ah trust of beauty and discipline,
win me to wait, leaning on wheel
till feel of distance, cosmic rest
bursts from that bush of traffic glow.
Know how the driven, flagging hate,
the lateness, panic, haste to be foiled,
in soil of patient moment fades,
to raise red quince of heaven's bush
in hush before the traffic moves.

SUMMER MEADOW

A meadow scented and blurred by summer dusk,
with the last birds flying, the sable hills brought near,
and the mist moving low and cool from the river,
gathering about the knees of a few old trees
quiet and lingering, at meadow's center; and the clear
high sky straight overhead; and sleep
not far; and a murmur among the old trees' leaves. . . .

this is quite similar to a few widows,
pleasant and old, who have spent fine lives,
often grieving for good husbands and better times,
who now gather at the center of the meadow
to murmur politely, to draw their shawls
close about withered necks, and remark on the cool

mild evening, avoiding reference to husbands dead,
speaking only of dew, and blackberries, and violet hills.
the trival things that linger, that are easily said.

What are the men doing in that field,
naked as winter sky,
and all the trees bent one way frozen?
Have they chosen to die rather than steel
the blood to struggle? Have they stripped the eye
of hope and crumbled the walled flesh down,
and burned the clothes from mortal shoulders
in order that gentle mercy of freezing may take,
may melt, may vitiate and drown
the will unable to declare
the simple act of honor:
indignation at usurper's power,
a decent hate
for the disciplines of terror
only imposed, discerned,
and yielded to of late?

His belt's an adder tamed to the hearth of power,
dropped out of courts of stars and taken
and fed to the muscled waist, the hour
when the scarred pole by the spur is bitten
and the voice-and-comfort keeper mounts to heaven.

Scabbard for awl and pliers, coiled copper wire
burning alive as Mercury's helmet curve:
he may cover his naked head with canvas dark
and sear the flesh of earth's metal with blazing stars;
or buckled to pole lean out on the wind's arm,
revolving with light, balanced on atom's core,
teaching the cable to succor mortal from harm,
giving the wire the sounds secret and fair
that swim from volcanic time, that tremble and stir,
that move as love, that leap the measured arc
between man's knowing and his yearning's fire.
And spaced in hamlet rooms, sundered and dim,
speakers and listeners, lonely and groping, become
fused to single shining through fingers of one
tuned to infinity's music — renascent through him.

We take this shining with us upon the street:
this mechanism housed to crisp our bread;
it flashes from our eyes for those we greet;
glitters, a morning crown, on lifted head.

Like any communion plate we hold it forth,
marking the sacred wheat to swell the vein.
Yet this new silver is worth
all centuries of pain,

for, while precise it ticks the leisured meal,
it gives us time to smile, to pray, prepare
for coming tasks, to feel
the ripe truth warming there.

CHANGED

I saw a man turned into money:
His head became a bank vault door
in which the wheels were seen to hurry,
the valves were heard to quaintly purr.

The breast was soft as brown purse leather
in which the bones were solid coin.
The bullion heart, held fast forever,
fed stocks and bonds through copper veins.

Lithe arms of greenbacks wound to cable
clasped lover and tomb and mortal tower;
with special joy reached to inveigle
the tender child with twist of power.

And looking down, I saw, amazed,
that the reproductive organs set
in wax and most conspicuously placed,
were nothing more than cancelled checks.

Fire is racing at the tips of grasses,
down slopes of brush and gullies of raw wind;
its body is the shadow of dark kisses
taken of earth by sun's eternal mind.

But at the verge of columbine it wearies,
before azalea's trumpet cry it holds;
fire curves and passes; beauty, its ageless quarry,
transforms the flame to fragrance, smoke to gold.

At night when cool, when cool the good rain comes
and seeks to fall more swiftly, and fails, and returns
to gray heaven, and heat hangs like a bruised plum
on the bough of windlessness, and the cricket's chirr
is muted; now, strange like an amiable scarecrow puzzled
by an old charm, the boy on a bicycle passes,
his shirt sweat-drenched, eyes odd, hair frizzled
with swimming and heat; aimless; his bike pedal flicking grasses
that grow tall, leaning, by the crooked wooden fence . . . .

Then, faint, but longed-for and pleasant as arms of a lover,
the spice of meadow mint enfolds the heart,
frail and ghostly, but true as wild bird's hover,
and the boy, not knowing why, feels the throat's gate
break wide with joy, and rising on pedals, flings
his weight at distance, and speeds on evening's wings.

What have we left together on the summer skies,
O red-winged blackbird crying in the sedges?
What streamer of immortal song, what cries
of red eternal daring, what bright pledges?
None can decipher what our joy inscribed,
red of your wing and leap of my kindled blood,
high on the looming air and low on the tide
of running water urging to full flood.
Let the black banners of the autumn cloud
snap in the wind, and let the snows roar over;
ever and ever will the earth be proud
and air be honored where our singing hovered.

III

❧ *The Thawing Fire*

1932-1949

EARLY MORNING BUS IN AUTUMN

Teach, then, faces alert to bend
athwart the windows of the autumn bus,
above the nerveless hand too frail to sin,
above newspapers thick and cold with lust;

teach! — what does the child within the womb
say to the leaf whirled by an engine's hurry?
What do the blue fumes write upon the tomb
of one more city day embalmed in fury?

Teach! face of student grooved to groaning rut
of lucubration and tormented urge. . .
The insufficient check blown in the mind's street
scrapes down through elms where rust and glory merge.

And workman, eyes flung windy and absorbed
against the blank stone of the leaning hour,
topple, and tell the dust what glinting gourd
swings on the porch of hope, gutted and sour.

Bold bronze he gleams
in hot sun-streams
of morning gold.
Metallic bright
in mulberry tree
he burns with light,
plucks storm-dark fruit,
flings into flight
round, liquid note.

O pirate singer,
O mulberry lover,
naked as metal,
you warm song-bringer! —
your body a sword
hammered by rapture,
your rippling word
delight beyond capture;
metal and madness,
plunder and power,
shining of armor,
soft glow of flower;
warrior incongruous:
lustful in hunger,
angry in brightness,
yet child heart of wonder,
love song of lightness.

SUNSET AND IMMORTALITY

Cloud and branch bathed in that fire,
that lavender, that thin and crystal pink
of cold reflection welling from the brink
of outer mountains, where, past steel-blue snow,
past last desire,
the lava rock of sun rolls down to dark.
Not as the sun or the winter mountain will we die,
not as color washed over cloud and mute bough;
but noble and stark
as figures in white hoods,
with our breath rolling white under sky,
we will walk out of this world,
past the white and desolate landscape, beyond where the steel plow
of mortal effort folds the curved snow high.

The cold of His resolve will be in us, the color of white truth
will sear from out of us what was uncouth,
will fork outward, cutting interstellar night.
In that motion, free-striding, upright,
we will not need the shadow of time,
the sunset's color or cry;
we shall be our own and His light.

Through the long orchard of a childhood dream,
under the blossom-loaded branches of the cherry,
the hunting cat moves with a rippling gleam,
parting the grass with muscled shoulder, rippled and furry.
Green core to golden eye, love shadowy and late
under the hot frost of that glancing look —
this is the cat that will crouch, and spring, and sate
the tendoned beast in him, and then at my gate
will yowl with murmured penitence. I at my book
will hear, and let him in. Then, later, curling
at window ledge, the wise smile cupping the jowl,
he will murmur his sly love, letting hate
sink down with embered glow through memory's grate,
knowing the moon will return with freedom, with howl
of fighters over the wild grass, and soft sound purling
under the shadowy vines where the lovers wait.

Through all the winding years of childhood moves
this tawny cat I loved, and watched, and fed,
and heard above the sound of sleet and snow,
prowling the world, while I lay warm in bed.
No night is dark, no swollen wind of autumn blows
without my hearing, far, and sad, and wild —
yet filled with all my longings too — that cry
horrid and bestial, murmured, and loving, and mild;
and yet I knew, I knew though still a child
that under the shadowy gold of the fur there glowed
the lava and the molten force of worlds
that lived at time's beginning, curved my sky

with sunburst, made the heart throb in the necks of girls,
and drove me through a world of beauty hungrily.

Gold cat immortal, parting the dew-bright grass,
crossing the windy orchards of years, hot life in your eye,
thanks for the furtive friendship, the hours of youth,
when under your savage voice sang the music of truth,
when the urge of the beast for love lay under the glass
of your green-gold watching. Even as I,
you knew the fight, the claw, the smell of blood.
Thanks for that lesson — that beauty molded in motion
and locking the hunger of flesh with the earth and the ocean
and all things lonely and lost under mortal sky.

Let this tree live, thought the child,
let the apples on this one tree never die.
And when winter came, and the cool mild
dark of autumn paled out of heart and sky
and the fruit had fallen,
lo! on that one tree the apples hung
still red, still naked and wild,
glowing against snow, like a sonata sung
by angels of a new angelic age,
like the crimson script on a page
torn from a lost book of miracles.

Dawn-flushed and young,
the apples gleamed in their ice, and swung
to the cold harp-thrum of the wind,
and the child walked through frozen orchard air
where the fruit of all other trees had fallen
and all other trees were leafless and sullen,
and saw the boughs of that tree softly aflame
with a color immortal, saw that his tiny prayer
had fixed against time one instant,
had kept one thing the same,
beyond all touch, perhaps, past others' knowing,
but sure, within his arch of faith,
an image fixed in memory's glowing
and heaven's grace.

FORMER HOMELAND

Beholding how each day must be the same
from the cockpit of waking to the fallen body of night,
the hope that maybe this former homeland has not changed
hurled on the gravel of knowing that fury is late,
and bushes grow on the mouth, and the path is strange,
and old fields grow thistle and sumac, and the dry air
crushes its hot mouth upon the ruins of barns
seeking to suck the past, the life once there
out of the ragweed and sumac, the rock and the worm . . .

hoping that maybe at this turn some love will spew
fair as the convulsion of loins in lover's grip
out of the orchards untended, a fount of the nervous and new,
some perfect apple from black disease, a wind
light with young voices of haytime where meadows now grow to
        seed,
recalling the hate and betrayal, the like-minded friends
who bent with me happy at strawberry slopes now underbrush-
        blind,
those who loved me, then found me too different, and fled . . .

wandering alone in the pits of dead shovels and gleam
gone from the pick, and the rusted frames for fire
to boil the sap from maples whose scars are so aged and deep
that my finger no longer can trace where the bright bit tore,
I yearn suddenly for the graves of the known, the ones
familiar or alien who knew better than I
that death is preferable to what man has done
to the skin and blood of justice, the bones of hope —
those who wisely yielded, or without choosing, died . . . .
I wish for the litany of their infinite silence and dark,

the length of their coldness pressed to the cold of my calm,
and no more war, and no more futile sallies
upon the breast of power whose pulse must last
till many more than I know and cry fury
and lance the veins and let the terror bleed
whose weight lay on the poor, the duped, the weak.
It would be best revolt to cheat life, and sleep.

But suddenly, in ruins of personal years, —
the havoc of man's cities, echoing vast,
mounts on the lacerated sky, the crowding fears
of self, the cellar-holes of an unconscious youth;
and on the bodies of the killed and the unkowing
I rise firmer in flesh than Lazarus to do
what is for future, out of invisible roots,
with strength made manifold out of the wild growing
of structures still too deep for grass to hear,
of days more friendly than the friends that were.

TELEPHONE WIRES IN WINTER

They sing as the burnt stars sing
And the flame-throated bird,
Wires from mouth to mouth,
Bearing the lovely wing
Of the human word.
Against the haunted blue of winter noon
Strung like the cold, thin arteries of song,
They can seem like death or serpents to a child,
They can seem like towers and a gong.
Eyes lifted, child face waiting,
Hearing that low, cold buzzing, as though a bee
Born out of ice and green-glazed snow,
Were floating through that space, through wires that flow
With fire entranced, with words from other worlds,
Swift and eternal, emerald and pearl.

Scaling dark walls to find a nest in heaven,
crawling stark rock with fingers bloody and raw,
he saw the vultures of remembered acts scale down,
poison-eyed, their claws the facts he thought forgotten;
and strange to say, they came from the cloud-cairn,
the very range where high and safe he thought to find
a nest of peace, gold-dark and warm, where fear
could not pursue. And now caught there, he saw the storm of
    feathers,
the beaks open and clipped; he saw the x-ray eyes gleaming,
and weak with sudden knowledge, he tumbled from the cliff of
    skies, earthward.

We are Egyptian dead —
procession underground —
the dust-enshrouded head,
the gray hands strictly wound
in thongs to keep erect
the empty bodies swaying —
mouths shaped to frozen sound,
eyes beyond hope or dread.

Volcanic undertone
pours from the funeral wheel —
the nether spirits' moan,
the gods who bend to seal
the lips of pyramids,
who rush us blindly down,
down through the vaults of stone,
past votive alcoves lit
with torchlight pale as bone.

Will we come to the dark river?
Will the swift wheels go under?
Will Isis, the strange giver,
blur the black wheels of thunder,
blend us with the void?
And will our bodies float
with faces turned to sky,
staring like Harold Lloyd,
wrapped in a Chaplin coat?

After death I shall surely see this red,
The color of alder berries against the gray
Of oak and maple, and the sombre day
Burning with misty coldness overhead.
After I leap the wall in heaven, and turn
The tall shrubbery, and pause to see
What this new country has for me,
I shall feel suddenly a color burn
Out of the light that fills the orchards of air,
And mist of Connecticut hills brought in from the sea
Will blow on my forehead, the oaks of my youth will be there.
And fixed against gentle gray of tree
And further gray of swamp and winter stream
That red — small jewels of eternity,
And rich and warm like blood that beats in dreams,
That fills our love with sweetness. Certainly
The Christ who walks the stairway deep
Within the towers of our hope,
Knows in his love what beauties we should keep,
Which of those mortal things for which we grope
Is true and worthy to go past the sleep
Of dying and be with us still.
Surely, if symbols of our growth and pain
Will live again to the touch, for further giving,
I will see alder and oak and winter again,
With a sound of carols, a sky that will soon be snowing.
Red of the alder, shining in misty cold,
With the mountain holly, the princess pine, and the bay,
The hemlock with small tight cones, all tucked in the fold
Of the big wreath hung on the door for Christmas day —

Yours is the red of life and the further living,
Blood of our Christ that in us beats and yearns
For joy and richness here, for the eager giving
That in that other country safe returns
In beauties known and loved, in shapes that show
How much we learned, how much we still must grow,
In mists, and seasons, and in touch that burns.

Brown, crumbled stone and the long slant of land,
mimic voices of silence in the thick web of sky;
here the thin roots weave under me, the poised land
rocks on the thrust of night and the cold bat blows by.
Curious leans the gaunt bough of the pine,
caught in the lucid wash of stars dimmed and drowned;
hepaticas we picked, boulders we leaned upon
crushed and rebellious in the dark tomb of ground.
No upward going now, no slow return;
hounds are forever calling in the late death of days;
love burned in this shadow and again will burn
when Orion flashes steel and the Pleiades ablaze
wing down on younger hearts, set fresh for hope
within this curve of calm, this buried slope.

Where is the wooden gate that opened in
on pine dusk and forgetfulness and hushed breath?
Little we knew of sorrow or the sense of sin
that, upward writhing to the throat of age,
tightens itself with greater strength than death.
Down this same pebbled way, past barbed wire bent
by cattle blundering, under this rubble
the woodchuck sick for refuge, the hedgehog sorely spent
hear in the black of trees the wings of trouble;
and human love, with tendrils of remorse,
coils in the hearts of new ones taking this way,
thinking perhaps this is a different course,
this place secure, this night immune to day.

Remember how the trees walked in the light —
that pale light out of lonely, twilight sky;
remember how you turned to me in fright,
saying, such trees must come from those who die —

out of each grave, a tree so quiet and sad
with the scars on the bent face and the eyes shining,
dead and yet dreamingly awake.
We watched the trees and saw them cross the lake,
great-shouldered, silent, with the dust of death
gleaming on neck and arms. Heaven must make
these trees to walk for us, you said,
to show how great and noble are the dead.

There will be similar people walking,
skirts shifting where the eye can run at will on flesh
inwardly where the mind stares.
There will be identical caresses, hot stumbling hands,
a breast that bares
round whiteness to a moon swimming
in passionate lands
of cloud and sky.
Certainly there is nothing shocking in a cry
smothered and late.
All these girls pass the same curve of the shore
each year, each night. New men will wait,
scanning the girls' bodies moving under faces,
flipping their cigarettes into the lake:
"Whaddya say, babe, wanna go places?"
Because you are not there any more,
do not think the air is any less soft,
or the water gone or the lake gone from the shore.
Some of the ones you kissed have grown older,
but they taught others before they went:
there is still a shoulder
with the dress pulled back,
under enormous-shadowed trees,
breasts still warm and slack,
thighs gripped with knees.
Certainly it would be pleasant to return,
but the difference mixed with the sameness
is much too difficult to learn.

THE BIRDS OF AUTUMN

The birds of autumn are gray and lonely things.
With sorrow in their eyes and quiet wings
They circle over empty oaks and slant away
Into the cold and dying light of day.
And time seems held a moment by their flight:
There is no autumn and there is no night;
Only the movement of their wings, the chill
Which stiffens every leaf and locks the hill
In silence which no mortal sound can break.
Some of the sadness of my heart is there,
Hung on those distant wings, bathed by the air
Which flows from mountains they are flying to.
O birds of autumn, lonely and too few,
How can you carry what I cannot bear?

I should like to be in the black lake now,
Under the ice, with my face to the sky.
I would feel the sweet clean cold of the water,
I could look up and see the skaters go by
Through the white, fine ice, the fragile curve
Of the blades biting down, the long, lovely swerve
Of a woman's body, the charge of a man
With quicker strokes and a pounding sound.
I shall go back to the lake, if I can,
Sometime before I die.
I should rather lie
There than underground.
I should rather be buried in water I loved,
Black under ice. The cold of it sealing me.
My face to the sky.

The owner of this city has been more than kind
and tender in his wishes for us all.
I saw him pasting bank notes on the blind,
hiding the dead-from-hunger behind a wall.

I saw a street car with bumpers of velour
run over frightened people most considerately:
the bones broke softly, and a velvet sewer
received the bodies — buried without fee.

I saw the needy naked in department stores
placed in a bronze globe dewy with perfume
which whirled them with subdued and pleasant roar
till they forgot their need of board and room.

I saw the starving sorrowed-for and loved
by a long procession of the richly clad
who touched thin, dying bodies with their gloves,
asked for a priest, slowly removed their hats.

The factory owner, compassionate and able,
saw that the hand torn by the new machine
was wrapped in linen napkins from his table,
a note sent to the workman's wife who grieved.

The owner of these owners, wherever he was,
could not be seen, but he was more than good:
on the prone body of each unemployed
he placed a vase of flowers to serve as food.

Open the pure door of that summer air
and see again gold dog loping through heat,
past blueberry bush and orange-paintbrush fur
toward aegis of desire, the depthless lake.

Tempered with sadness, slanted on turquoise sky,
ready to yield the soul to summer thunder,
grave animal, long-nosed, lank, and too-sharp-thighed,
racing the ball of sun, the dry earth's tinder,
brushing the grass whose cool touch is a dream,
fighting for breath where rocky hill-tops steam. . .

Did you ever reach that water? Did I ever learn
what God-ordained content is in a thirst slaked?
My blood stretched with your running gold to where light burned
incredibly like Arthur's shield on hammered lake.

You paled from sight. Only when ice hung sharp
its coat-of-mail upon the lake's side,
did I, dead spent from skating swift and far,
bend to the hole cut by fisherman's pike,
and in the fury cold of water aching the throat,
welling dark against my grateful lips,
see all that you had found, whether gaining or lost,
whether reaching water or carried on hopeless ships
beyond your summer's thirst, and death's frost.
Seeking or finding, prayer is the self made quick.

Copper penny shone
On flat stone,
On brick burnished by light:
Late lonely faces and the lone
Sun standing bright
On windy winter skylines,
Burnished stars
And copper hatred in the eyes of one
Tall, terrible, and bare.

. . . and light, this firelight on a copper face,
Red as the sandstone seeping under walls
Where silence and cold sunlight falls,
And for long years no human face
Has known the thawing fire, nor coin has bit
The hot young hand that clutches it.

Now with you fully mine there are tongues of fire that enshroud
     me,
there are bells of pearl that swing from your limbs and din in my
     blood,
there are tempests of wind that fall from your hair to becloud me,
and all of my senses are lost in an uttermost flood.

Ah, fire and frost of your kiss, ah, voice of your crying! —
forever and ever I live in the single touch of your finger;
I feel and remember God, I am birth from the ashes of dying;
on the wings of your flesh I am bright and immortal flying
at heaven's blazing gate, looking back to the earth's cold moon.

Out of the quick of your heart pursue and succor me soon,
out of the springs of your tenderness water the pores of my
     yearning,
out of your tropical valleys curved in the snows of delight
send the thin silvery arrows of sweetness to pierce my burning,
cover the throes of my flesh with a mantle of white.

Do you think they will ever find us? We have turned the corner, we have passed through the tall brown sorrel, heart-swift as the brown of deer over mountain laurel.

They can never find us; we have hidden our love forever in the night-cool ferns of calmness where star fire burns, where the sunlight builds like coral the love's endeavor, and no one can hear what we say, not even the clever.

They can never follow. No custom or creed, no world-words inquiring can reach us here. We shall never heed the pollen blown from the meadows behind, nor remembrance's seed. We shall cut the young thought in the bark, and keep something separate, and talk in the dark, slow syllables such as the bloodroot bleed.

THE HARBOR LONGS FOR SHOUTING

They lived upon a mountain crowned with light,
Often descending, for they loved the sea;
They swam into the moonlight, naked, bright,
Swam in the breakers, swam through sparkling night,
Turned in the cool, dark waters lovingly.

They brought their fruit in barges gold and white,
And wood sweet-smelling, strong for bridge and spire;
Full-rigged they sailed, and staunch and quick for flight;
Glad their returning and the catching sight
Of roof-tops on the peaks, sweet their desire.

O ruddy racers, swimmers, mountain hearts,
You of the colored sail, the throaty cry,
The crooked roadways and the stumbling carts,
Breathing the raw salt air that heals and smarts,
Breathing the hill calm and the open sky,

What pathway have you left along the wave,
What hammer blow upon a crumbled stone?
The looming ocean moon has lost her slave,
The harbor longs for shouting. Tall and brave
Your last full sail has met the stars, alone.

He leans against the shed, the brown stem of his pipe hung down from features bled of all desire, all strength, the slow fire in the pipe bowl dead, his body sagging loose to all its length.

Nothing brings money any more: not milk nor apples nor the heavy store of harvests dragged away from earth to rot. Nothing he labors for and loves brings payments on the things he's bought. Only the cry of creditors breaks through his thought, stronger than his own child's crying, enduring longer than the battle fought by toil, more deathless than the purpose of the soil, alive with all his life and substance dying.

Nothing brings money any more. No need to ask for credit at the store, or separate the cream and go the rounds. What is this dream of profits? Dim and vague it sounds, and all connections seem undone. Who gets ahead from profits of the grower? No one living in his town. Does anyone? Who backs the credit of the store, and who backs them? And how far back does all this credit go? He does not know. He leans against the shed and bites the brown stem of his pipe and wonders why a man's love cannot be enough to buy the stuff to keep his loving, why a man's heartbreaking labor is not worth even the food and rest to keep him breathing after birth.

These goods I keep within my window-case
Are not the only reason for my store;
I offer men a friendly meeting-place
When leaves of autumn whirl about the door,
And when the deadly colds of winter come.
Sometimes I half forget they buy my wares
When faces glow that have been dark and glum,
And when, between the lips that have been dumb,
My best cigar draws forth an old man's cares.

Back of the store, among the storage piles,
The fat stove mocks the winter with its heat:
There sallow Deacon Kendall stands, and smiles,
And there the woodsmen lounge and dry their feet;
Old Andrew's teeth and cheek are wedged apart
With cut plugs bigger than his aging heart.

My store is known to you by ounce and pound,
But that is not the only value there;
Come out into the rear and look around:
See how the snowflakes melt from shocks of hair,
And how the gloves and leather jackets steam;
Hear youngsters boast and older men explain,
Mark how the thin will flush, the fat will beam,
How wood is known according to its grain,
And distance measured by the swiftest team.
Here is a nourishment that thaws the cold
And keeps the limbs and wits from growing old.

This town will never live, you know it well: the deer that wander
    on the hill through shifting snow look down on chimneys
    huddled in the chill of night. These homes will go.
Strange, broken flight of a winter bird crosses the moon, dies on
    the air like the long-fading cry of a loon, like the failing word,
    raggedly spoken, faintly heard.
Somewhere in frozen mosses, thin and spare like broken crosses,
    the bones that built these walls, the flesh that stirred, will lie
    beneath the cloven hoof of deer still wandering here.

I know the shape of every head in town;
At all town meetings I can mark with pride
How smooth the necks are, how the hair thins down
Above the collar and on either side.
Henry has bumps like eggs behind his ear,
And Martin's skull is broad and flat behind;
Each one I recognize from front and rear
According to the cover for his mind.
It's not my business how their suits are worn,
Nor what the fashion is in dress and hose;
But when the hair is ragged and forlorn,
And when the chin with stubble overflows,
I think with fear upon the human lot
If they were as they are, and I were not.

CERTAINTY

These leaves will gleam forever. These leaves, these leaves
We put our hands to in the thirsty noon.
There is no end save what the mind conceives,
And what the heart relinquishes too soon.
Dust of the roadway settles to the grass,
And what we stirred is still; but on the bough
These leaves will gleam, nor will they ever pass
While we retain the strength we summon now.
Hot noon is here, my love, and whitened sky
Chokes us with chaff of ages and of change;
But close against us shines the full reply
To every longing. No, it is not strange
That we may keep a brightness that must go,
For we are surer than the things we know.

THE AUTHOR

With the appearance of his *Collected Poems,* George Abbe marks his fiftieth birthday and nearly thirty years as a poet, novelist, editor, and teacher.

Although he was born in New England and has lived much of his life there, Mr. Abbe's poetic themes transcend regional boundaries and are universal to our times. He expresses his beliefs and feelings with passionate conviction: his concern for the individual in an ever more systematized world; his lyrical sensitivity to Nature; his awareness of God. He is recognized today as one of America's outstanding poets, and in 1956 won the coveted Shelley Memorial Award, presented by the Poetry Society of America.

Since his first book appeared in 1938, four novels and five volumes of Mr. Abbe's poetry have been published. His poems are familiar to readers of *The Atlantic, Saturday Review,* and many other periodicals; he has recorded his work for the Library of Congress, the Harvard Series of Modern Poets, and Folkways Corp.

In his youth a student of the late Stephen Vincent Benet, Mr. Abbe is now teaching younger poets and writers himself. He has taught at Yale, Columbia, Mt. Holyoke, Iowa, Wayne State, and at other universities. He is presently Poet-in-Residence at Russell Sage College.

Also widely-known as a lecturer and reader, George Abbe has served on the staffs of writers' conferences in Idaho, Texas, Connecticut, Ohio, and New Hampshire. He is an editor of the Book Club for Poetry.

DATE DUE